Planting schemes from

FRANCES LINCOLN   Published in association with The National Trust

SISSINGHURST

TONY LORD

Frances Lincoln Ltd
4 Torriano Mews, Torriano Avenue
London NW5 2RZ
www.franceslincoln.com
In association with The National Trust (Enterprises) Ltd
36 Queen Anne's Gate
London SW1H 9AS

Planting Schemes from Sissinghurst
Copyright © Frances Lincoln Ltd 2003
Text and photographs copyright © Tony Lord 2003
First Frances Lincoln edition 2003

Designed by Caroline Hillier

British Library Cataloguing-in-Publication data
A catalogue record for this book is available from the British Library
ISBN 0 7112 1788 2
Printed and bound in China
9 8 7 6 5 4 3 2 1

HALF-TITLE In the Nuttery, pale lavender *Anemone
nemorosa* 'Robinsoniana' meanders through white
bluebells and *Geranium sylvaticum* 'Mayflower',
accompanied by Mrs Robb's bonnet (*Euphorbia
amygdaloides* var. *robbiae*) and Bowles' golden grass
(*Milium effusum* 'Aureum'). This charming and
intimate tapestry needs relatively little maintenance.

TITLE PAGE Outside the South Cottage in spring,
wallflowers, tulips and *Euphorbia griffithii* 'Dixter'
provide colour among burgeoning foliage. Though
the varied shapes and shades of leaves are
attractive in themselves, the warm-hued flowers
need to be used in sufficient quantity if the
interplay of colours is to be effective.

Contents

When I was asked in 1993 to write *Gardening at Sissinghurst*, it seemed like a dream come true: there was a complex and fascinating story to unravel, a tale of three parts, only the first of which had been fully covered in earlier books. The history of how diplomat and politician Harold (later Sir Harold) Nicolson and his wife, the writer and poet Vita Sackville-West, had found the ruinous fragments of Sissinghurst and come to make their home and garden there, a romantic and inspiring story, merited retelling. Then there was the story of the survival of Sissinghurst, through the beneficence of Harold and Vita's son, Nigel, and the dedication and skill of a succession of outstanding gardeners under the National Trust. This in itself is remarkable: it is hard enough to achieve the transition from a family garden with about 6,000 visitors a year to a world famous one seen annually by some 200,000 people; to do so without significantly eroding its character and charm is a remarkable accomplishment. Lastly, there is the story of the planting, the subject of this book: what has been planted where, to create the distinctive Sissinghurst style of planting, and how it is maintained. The chance to roam around the garden with my camera in early mornings, before the visitors or even the gardeners had arrived, was a welcome bonus that gave me an opportunity to analyse what I saw.

A brief outline of the story of the garden and its planting is needed to set the scene. Vita bought Sissinghurst in 1930, when she was thirty-eight, Harold was forty-three and their sons Ben and Nigel were sixteen and thirteen. The decision to buy may have been influenced by the realization that this would be a good place to garden: many of the enclosures they so loved to plant were already there. Before any of the buildings were habitable, they set to work on the garden. Vita set out their roles and objectives in an article in the *Journal* of the Royal Horticultural Society: 'I could never have done it by myself. Fortunately I had, through marriage, the ideal collaborator. Harold Nicolson should have been a garden-architect in another life. He has a natural taste for symmetry, and an ingenuity for forcing focal points or long-distance views where everything seemed against him, a capacity I totally lacked. We did, however, agree entirely on what was to be the main principle of the garden: a combination of long axial walks . . . and the more intimate surprise of small geometrical gardens opening off them, rather as the rooms of an enormous house would open off the arterial corridors. There should be the strictest formality of design, with the maximum informality in planting.'

Thus the garden at Sissinghurst was the product of the creative tension between two different personalities, the Apollonian order and control of Harold's formal design versus the Dionysian exuberance and excess of Vita's planting. However, it is simplistic to assume that Harold acted solely as designer while Vita provided all the planting: Vita influenced Harold's design ideas, occasionally even ruling out some of the more ambitious ones, while Harold bought plants himself, and not just for the Lime Walk which he called My Life's Work.

In 1932 they moved into Sissinghurst, though the living accommodation was not completed until 1935. By 1937 most of the structure of the garden was in place. With the departure of several of the gardeners to join the armed forces, the war years saw something of a decline, but this was reversed with the return of the gardeners in 1946. 1950 saw the creation of the White Garden. However, by the late 1950s Vita's health was failing and horticultural standards showed a temporary decline. Though it may have seemed freer and more romantic than ever to most visitors, professional horticulturists who saw it at this time felt that the garden might have reached the point of no return: freedom and informality were about to give way to chaos and, before long, oblivion. However lovely the appearance of the garden, it was unlikely to survive without monumental and sustained effort and the utmost skill. Sissinghurst in the late 1950s needed a miracle if it was to survive.

The arrival in 1959 of Pam Schwerdt and Sibylle Kreutzberger as head gardeners was a happy chance that proved to be Sissinghurst's salvation. Trained at Waterperry Horticultural School, Oxfordshire, they worked with Vita until her death in 1962, long enough to know her planting style and preferences well (though they received few instructions from Vita and almost none from Harold). Their industry and endlessly critical approach to their work ensured that weeds were eliminated, soil fertility improved and longer-flowering or superior plant varieties used to replace any that did not pull their weight. They brought further refinements to the training and pruning of roses and wall plants and to the staking of herbaceous plants, including making a small plantation of hazels for production of suitable brushwood. In all of this, perhaps their greatest challenge was to extend the season of display into the autumn. Vita had always lamented that the garden became dull by mid-July. By using tender perennials, in particular, Pam and Sibylle managed to ensure that visitors, whenever they arrived, would find the garden looking beautiful and full of interest; at the same time they helped bring about a way of planting for late summer and autumn effect that is now widely used by gardeners around the world.

Vita left Sissinghurst to Nigel, the more rural of her two sons, who took over the running of the garden. Faced with heavy death duties that could not be met out of capital, all of which had been invested in the repair of the buildings and the making of the garden, Nigel's preferred option was to offer the castle and garden to the Treasury in part payment of duty, on the understanding that the property would be transferred to the National Trust. Vita had left Nigel a letter saying that she realized what the financial problems would be and would understand if he were to choose this option. Within not much more than a month of Vita's death, with Harold's knowledge and consent, Sissinghurst was offered to the National Trust.

Five years of negotiations followed, throughout which the transfer to the Trust was far from being a foregone conclusion: some of its Gardens Committee felt that Sissinghurst was 'not one of the great gardens of England'; one member, Vita's friend Alvilde Lees-Milne, disagreed strongly: 'I and thousands of others put Sissinghurst way above such places as Sheffield Park. It is not only romantic and intimate, as well as full of interest, it also happens to have been created by a great English poet and writer. To my way of thinking it is everything a garden should be.' She won the day: Sissinghurst was transferred to the Trust on 13 April 1967.

Harold Nicolson died at Sissinghurst on 1 May 1968. In that same year, the National Trust and the gardeners embarked upon a major programme of work that was to preserve its built features for generations to come and equip it for ever-increasing numbers of visitors. Walls were repointed and roofs mended; uneven paving, most of it laid on bare soil, was reset on a solid base throughout the garden, removing toe-tripping changes of level; grass paths, where they were regularly worn away by the thousands of visitors, were replaced with brick or stone, to Nigel's designs. The scale of such projects would have been beyond all but the most affluent and determined of private owners. Otherwise, the gardeners were pleased to find that they were allowed to get on with maintaining the garden as they had done for the previous nine years, with the minimum of interference.

In 1984, a catalogue of the garden's plants was compiled by the Trust. This showed that, although many shrubs and wall plants remained where they were in Vita's time, overall less than one third of the plants then at Sissinghurst had grown there in 1959. In the course of a single year, about a third of the plants in an intensively gardened area such as the Purple Border may be moved or replaced. The constant refining of the planting, removing unworthy varieties and adding good new ones, has continued since Vita's death, as she would have wished, though the soft and abundant style of her planting remains unchanged. There is probably no other garden anywhere in which, over the last forty years, so many successful plant associations have been assembled. Many assume that all the garden's most beautiful plant associations were created by Vita, any less successful ones by the gardeners. This is a fallacy: though the style and spirit of Vita's garden remain, the planting has been so frequently and so comprehensively rearranged that few of its individual groupings have endured; the associations we see, though in Vita's style, are predominantly the creation of the gardeners.

Pam and Sibylle retired in 1991, passing on the post of head gardener to Sarah Cook, who had worked with them at Sissinghurst from 1984 to 1988. Sarah now combines this role with that of property manager, co-ordinating various other activities at Sissinghurst, including the shop, restaurant, visitor services, functions and building projects, with the running of the garden. Alexis Datta is now the assistant head gardener, providing an interchange of opinions with Sarah analogous to that between Harold and Vita and subsequently Pam and Sibylle. Sarah is the first to admit that her own methods of gardening and planting differ somewhat from those of Pam and Sibylle, though she is committed to keeping the traditions of Sissinghurst and its spirit intact.

Three happy circumstances have ensured the survival and enrichment of the garden since its creators' time. One is the foresight and continued generosity of Nigel Nicolson. The second is the single-minded perseverance, industry and professionalism of the gardeners. Not only have they kept alive the planting and the spirit of the garden; they have also quietly but effectively changed the way we all plant, particularly in their use of tender perennials to provide late colour. Thirdly, the involvement of the National Trust has given support for the gardeners, expertise for maintenance of the fabric, access and facilities for visitors and a guarantee of Sissinghurst's survival. It is doubtful whether any other organization would have had both the sensitivity and the resources to keep the garden so alive, to be enjoyed by so many.

This is not a labour-saving garden: as Sarah points out, 'The only way to achieve a garden like this is by constant hard work, endless observation and criticism.' Yet this will not deter any of us from enjoying Sissinghurst. And even if we cannot imitate it exactly in our own gardens, we can learn much from it and copy at least a few of its plant associations, practical techniques or colour schemes. The garden is kept alive by constant reworking and replanting so that it is never the same on successive visits; there is always something to see there that captivates.

Spring Bulb Displays

White and Yellow Narcissi

Tulips with Spring Plants

Erythroniums and Crown Imperials

Fritillaries and Bluebells

Snakeshead fritillaries, grape hyacinths and scillas in the Lime Walk, an imposing garden room that is like a long gallery set with pictures of the most brilliant spring flowers.

A tapestry of spring flowers gladdens the heart of any gardener. At Sissinghurst, nowhere demonstrates more clearly what a well-chosen and cleverly managed bulb planting can achieve than the Lime Walk. Here, a dazzlingly intense informal display of spring flowers is set within a strongly architectural framework: the structure of the pleached limes makes up for the shortness of the bulbs, which fill a wide and spacious walk. As many bulbs have blooms in bright primary colours, the effect needs to be softened by a good proportion of white and cream flowers; white narcissi, snakeshead fritillaries, wood anemones and *Erythronium* 'White Beauty' all fill this role, with statuesque crown imperials providing strong yellow or orange accents at intervals. Shorter plants, including erythroniums and many blue muscari and scillas, act as a foil for taller tulips and daffodils and the only remaining shrubs, bright carmine *Prunus tenella* 'Fire Hill'.

Terracotta pots are filled with forget-me-nots and Lily-flowered tulips, favoured for their shorter habit and less formal appearance. Tulip 'Red Shine' is usually chosen, its late flowers lasting as much as a month, although yellow 'West Point' has occasionally been used.

The bulbs are deadheaded and hand-weeded weekly while in flower; a good mulch makes weed control fairly easy. Left to die back after flowering, the foliage can be cut down and cleared by early summer. Diseased bulbs are removed while the plants are still showing.

As the bulbs' display is finishing, take some time to assess the season's effect – to see if there are any gaps or unsuccessful colour associations and companion plantings that could be improved next year and to order new bulbs and other plants to remedy any shortcomings. At Sissinghurst daffodils and anemones are potted as soon as they arrive to prevent them from drying out; tulips (treated with a fungicide to lessen the risk of damage by tulip fire fungus) and other bulbs are not planted until mid-autumn. For new bulb groups or those that need augmenting, bulbs are potted into 9cm/3½in pots or 12.5cm/5in pans, placed in an open frame and covered with 7.5cm/3in of crushed bark mulch to await spring planting. When bulb leaves appear, showing their positions, the new bulbs can be planted, filling the deficiencies noted the previous year. The pots and pans are of varying sizes, containing different numbers of bulbs, so that the shape of a group can be accurately amended and the density kept uneven for greater informality.

Early flowers can be worked throughout the entire depth of a border, as other parts of the garden at Sissinghurst show. In the Purple Border, tulips, such as 'Blue Parrot', 'Pandion', 'Dairy Maid' and 'Greuze', and biennial wallflowers occupy gaps which perennials fill later. For this to be effective you need substantial groups, as in the Cottage Garden, where behind tulip 'Georgette', maroon-purple 'Black Parrot' tulips are combined with *Euphorbia polychroma* 'Major' in front of wallflower 'Vulcan', *Trollius × cultorum* 'Superbus' and Siberian wallflowers, all in sufficient quantities to establish an interplay of colours from group to group.

Bulbs naturalized in long grass provide a different kind of informality. In the Orchard, snowdrops and *Crocus tommasinianus* thrive with snakeshead fritillaries and colchicums; numerous varieties of narcissi give a long flowering season, starting with lenten lilies and 'Soleil d'Or' and finishing with *N. poeticus*; and cream and white varieties leaven the yellows of abundant daffodils to avoid an all-too-even carpet of yellow.

LEFT Before the largest and most sumptuous tulips bloom, narcissi provide the mainstay of the display in the Lime Walk. White-flowered sorts help leaven the effect, while velvety Cowichan polyanthus provide rich bass notes beneath.

BELOW Large and brash daffodils would upstage the quiet charm of intricate and small flowers in subdued colours such as these gold-laced polyanthus, though miniatures such as *Narcissus* 'Sundial' make ideal companions.

Spring planting requires substantial groups in several different colours for the interplay between plants to be effective. At the entrance to the Rose Garden from the Lower Courtyard, pink Single Late Group tulip 'Clara Butt' and amethyst Lily-flowered tulip 'Maytime', pansies, the Atragene Group clematis 'Ruby' and *Berberis thunbergii* 'Rose Glow' are sufficient to initiate the Long Border's spring-to-autumn colour scheme. The tulips can be grown beneath the taller roses and between herbaceous plants and will have started to die back when the foliage of their companions unfurls. Each planting of tulips needs occasional 'topping up' with more bulbs of the same variety to ensure they produce enough colour to make a coherent scheme. The pansies will be replaced by bedding of annuals or tender perennials to continue the display into summer.

BELOW Fosteriana Group varieties such as 'Orange Emperor' are the earliest of the large-flowered tulips, blooming in the Lime Walk in early spring with *Scilla bifolia* and grape hyacinths.

RIGHT At the foot of the Lime Walk's hornbeam hedge, the tall Single Late Group tulip 'Greuze' continues the display into late spring, with snakeshead fritillaries, *Muscari latifolia*, narcissi and polyanthus.

LEFT The most imposing of spring bulbs, crown imperials (*Fritillaria imperialis*) add height and impact to spring planting such as this in the Lime Walk. *Leucojum aestivum* 'Gravetye Giant' furnishes in front.

BELOW The broad leaves of *Erythronium* 'Pagoda' provide a welcome contrast to the grassy leaves of muscari and snakeshead fritillaries, accompanied by anemones and polyanthus in the Lime Walk.

OVERLEAF An imposing group of *Fritillaria imperialis* 'Maxima Lutea' in the Lime Walk. In front, the ground below dwarf cherry *Prunus tenella* 'Fire Hill' is carpeted with *Erythronium californicum* 'White Beauty'.

ABOVE In the Lime Walk, hybrid pink bluebells and *Primula sieboldii* are used to extend the display into late spring, accompanied by myrtle spurge (*Euphorbia myrsinites*).

RIGHT A charming millefleurs tapestry in the Lime Walk, with elegant nodding bells of snakeshead fritillary in white and dusky purple standing above blue *Anemone apennina*, white *A. blanda* and grape hyacinths (*Muscari armeniacum*).

LEFT In the Lime
Walk, the dusky
maroon bells of
Fritillaria pyrenaica
could scarcely find a
more effective foil
than the acid yellow-
green flowerheads of
Euphorbia polychroma
'Major'.

RIGHT Along the
Moat Walk, the
common yellow
azalea (*Rhododendron
luteum*) contrasts
effectively with the
elegantly nodding
flowers of common
bluebell
(*Hyacinthoides non-
scripta*).

Climbers and Shrubs
for Walls and Frames

Clematis

Wisteria

Roses

Shrubs

The solution to clothing a wall sometimes lies in allowing a plant to trail from above. Here in the Lower Courtyard, *Lophospermum scandens* has been planted on a ledge towards the top of one of the walls, creating a cascade of wine-red bells.

Sissinghurst is blessed with many mellow brick walls, all of them fully used to house a varied array of climbers and wall plants. (Their crumbly mortar even allows a few species such as wallflowers and the charming shrubby *Convolvulus cneorum* to be grown directly in them.) Most gardens will have similar sites, whether on the house itself or around the garden's boundary, that can be used to full effect by following some of Sissinghurst's examples.

The choice of plants depends primarily on the aspect of the wall. If facing the sun, provided it is not inclined to the east where frozen shoots might thaw fatally quickly in spring, it will provide precious microclimates for plants that would be too tender to grow in the open garden. An east-facing wall will be in rain shadow and suited to plants liking dry conditions, though some such as roses might be more prone to diseases such as blackspot and mildew here. West-facing walls, particularly if inclined towards the sun, will be moister and suited to many different genera. Even walls facing away from the sun can be used for lovers of cool shade such as ivies, climbing hydrangeas, schizophragmas and *Pileostegia viburnoides*.

Success with wall plants depends on two tasks, both of them practised to perfection at Sissinghurst: pruning and training. To produce the maximum amount of bloom in the small space available to them, some pruning is usually necessary and the ideal techniques can be found in many authoritative books, differing for each individual sort of rose, clematis or other genus. However, such rigid rules are not always practical in a garden like Sissinghurst. Here the gardeners have had to bend the rules in ways that do not sacrifice the final result: pruning often has to be done in late autumn rather than early spring or summer. Training is also crucial, carried out as often as every ten days for clematis when they are in active growth. Many climbers benefit from having their stems trained in an almost horizontal position, encouraging them to produce numerous lateral flowering shoots. Climbers can be trained to taut galvanized wires running horizontally between vine eyes along the joints of the brickwork, though in the Top Courtyard, the many clematis there are held in place by pig wire, whose vertical strands prevent the clematis from slipping too far sideways. This avoids the kinking of the stems that can cause wounds through which clematis wilt disease can penetrate. The netting is wrapped over the top of the wall, letting the clematis hold on to the top of the wall without being blown forward to form a bulky and unsightly quiff as it approaches the coping.

Planting on a wall at the back of a border such as the Purple Border gives an invaluable means of continuing an effect such as a colour scheme upwards. The choice of wall shrub or climber can depend on the bulk needed: whereas a climber will usually be trained tightly against the wall, a wall shrub might create a 'bump' standing prominent from the wall. Several of these along the back of a border can provide a succession of planting bays and can diminish any appearance of rigid linearity. The choice of wall shrubs is considerable: something that would be too tender for the open garden, such as an azara or ceanothus, might be a popular choice, or perhaps something with handsome foliage, or enchanting fragrance to waft through an open window such as the *Magnolia grandiflora* in the Top Courtyard. And though we have been considering only the woody plants so far, annual climbers such as sweet peas and morning glories and herbaceous ones such as perennial peas will also have a role to play.

LEFT The medieval wall of the Moat Walk, ornamented at intervals with Adam-style lead urns, is further furnished with varied climbers, including wisterias, vines and clematis. All clematis bear their blooms with exquisite poise on delicate, wiry stems. The Viticella sorts, such as 'Alba Luxurians' here, are among the most charming and most useful, valuable especially for their late flowering. They need pruning almost to the ground each year, ideally in early spring, though at Sissinghurst the gardeners often find it more convenient to prune in late autumn. This annual removal of their stems allows them to be easily disentangled from any supporting shrub or companion climber with perennial woody stems such as a vine or rose. As the stems of the clematis grow back, they should be regularly trained out and tied in against their support to prevent the stems kinking at the base; the wounding that results from such kinks can allow entry of clematis wilt disease.

OVERLEAF In the Lower Courtyard, colours have been chosen to harmonize with nearby key plants, in this case *Magnolia liliiflora* 'Nigra', its flowers of rich pink with a vinous red reverse opening from upright buds borne like candles on a Christmas tree. Drifts of the Barnhaven strain of *Primula sieboldii* in pink and carmine intermingle with the dusky pink pendent flowers of dicentra. Above the entrance to the Rose Garden, the wall is lightly clad with swags of *Clematis × vedrariensis*; this is no mean feat for a climber that, like its parent *C. montana*, is prone to form itself into dense and inelegant masses in which the individual beauty of the flowers is lost in the sheer profusion of the blooms. This is achieved by spur-pruning all lateral shoots after flowering, analogous to the pruning of vines, espalier pears or apples, leaving only a couple of nodes from which the next year's flowers can be produced.

LEFT, ABOVE AND BELOW The curved wall at the head of the Rose Garden houses one of Sissinghurst's most memorable pieces of planting, with five *Clematis* 'Perle d'Azur' and two claret vines, *Vitis vinifera* 'Purpurea', spaced at intervals and trained to intermingle, a scheme implemented by the gardeners since Vita and Harold's time. The vines must be pruned in late autumn, so the clematis are tackled at the same time rather than in early spring, the usual time for pruning Late Large-flowered Group varieties. The shoots of both must be spaced out and tied in every ten days or so during May and June.

RIGHT Purple Late Large-flowered Group clematis 'Madame Grangé' and pink Texensis 'Duchess of Albany', trained to horizontal wires on the Rose Garden wall.

ABOVE Along the Moat Walk, *Wisteria brachybotrys* 'Shiro-kapitan' (syn. *W. venusta*) is held in place by wires on the top of the wall and protected from bird damage by black cotton threads. The creamy fumitory *Corydalis ochroleuca* grows in cracks in the wall.

RIGHT The view from the Orchard shows the bank of yellow azaleas growing on the far side of the Moat Walk.

The view from the Orchard obliquely across the Moat Walk to the statue of Dionysus. A border of *Symphytum caucasicum* contrasts with Vita's original plant of glistening white *W. brachybotrys* 'Shiro-kapitan'. Buds of later-flowering *W. floribunda* 'Alba' promise a spectacular display of 45cm/18in-long racemes. The wallflower *Erysimum* 'Bowles' Mauve', growing in the wall, pokes up into view, while on the far left pale-leaved *Elaeagnus* 'Quicksilver' towers above the wall, helping give enclosure to the walk when seen from below. Though wisterias are traditionally pruned two or even three times in the course of a year to encourage the ripening of flowering spurs, at Sissinghurst a simpler technique is used. In the last week of July or the first of August, new stems are cut back to two or three nodes. There will be little or no subsequent vegetative growth and each of these nodes should produce flowers the following spring. No later pruning is necessary, unless dead wood needs to be removed during winter.

ABOVE Climbing Hybrid Tea rose 'Meg' in the Top Courtyard on the sunny wall of the entrance range.

RIGHT The same wall with 'Meg' on the far left, *Ceanothus* 'Percy Picton' (right), red Climbing Hybrid Tea 'Allen Chandler' planted on both sides of the arch and Climbing Tea 'Gloire de Dijon' left of the arch.

LEFT, ABOVE and BELOW and RIGHT The Rambler rose over the central arbour of the White Garden (*R. mulliganii*, long misidentified as *R. longicuspis*) is smothered in bloom and strongly fragrant throughout mid-summer each year. Its vigour makes it hard to keep it to its allotted space. The normal rules for pruning Rambler and Climbing roses do not work at Sissinghurst: Ramblers cannot be pruned in late summer when the garden is crowded with visitors and Climbing roses on walls would interfere with work on the borders beneath if left until spring. Both sorts are pruned in late autumn, with no apparent ill effect or diminution of flowering.

In the south-east corner of the Top
Courtyard, two plants of *Viburnum plicatum*
f. *tomentosum* 'Lanarth', trained against the
walls, mask their rectilinearity with their
characteristic layered habit of growth. This
provides an altogether freer and more
romantic effect than would be achieved
with climbers, which would, by their very
nature, remain pressed fairly close to the
wall. For later effect, a wispy climber such
as a Texensis clematis, maurandya or
Rhodochiton atrosanguineus could be draped
over the wall shrub, a technique that is
perhaps especially useful in the case of
early-flowering wall shrubs with relatively
uninteresting foliage. Beneath, a border of
long-spurred columbines coincides in
flowering season with the viburnum.

ABOVE The trumpet vine (*Campsis radicans*) is secured to wires along the top of the Moat Walk's wall but is also able to scramble into *Elaeagnus* 'Quicksilver' behind, contrasting with its pale foliage.

RIGHT The vermilion flowers of flowering quince *Chaenomeles* × *superba* 'Knap Hill Scarlet' harmonize perfectly with the brickwork of Sissinghurst's entrance range. As with its relatives apples and pears, plentiful blooming depends on establishment of flowering spurs and ripening of the wood, achieved by summer pruning to shorten lateral shoots and remove excess stems.

LEFT *Rosmarinus officinalis* 'Sissinghurst Blue' is a variety that arose as a chance seedling in the tower steps during the mid-1950s and throve there in the lime mortar. Richer blue than common rosemary but slightly less hardy, it benefits from the shelter of a sunny wall.

RIGHT On a sunny wall in the Lower Courtyard, the powder-blue flowers of *Ceanothus × delileanus* 'Gloire de Versailles' combine with dainty blue *Clematis viticella* and agapanthus, leavened by white flowers of the Turkish hollyhock (*Alcea pallida*). The ceanothus is relatively hardy but repays its favoured position by long and copious flowering; the previous year's growth is pruned hard back to just two pairs of buds in early to mid-spring each year.

Colour in
Beds and Borders

Purple Hues

Sunset Colours

White and Silver

Extending the Season

Macleaya microcarpa and *Alstroemeria ligtu* hybrids in the Sunken Garden in the corner of the Lower Courtyard harmonize with the Tudor brick walls.

Sissinghurst's division into a series of rooms allowed each part of the garden to be planted in a different way and with a different range of colours. Every part of the spectrum is used: the Cottage Garden has the hot colours, from scarlet through yellow to yellow-green; in the Rose Garden cool colours predominate, crimson, magenta and mauve through to blue, though with touches of apricot, and yellow-green and lime green to add piquancy and prevent blandness; then there are the White Garden and the Purple Border. Elsewhere in the garden, the use of colour is less controlled: in the Lime Walk, primary colours predominate among the spring flowers, softened by plentiful white and cream; the Nuttery has no colour scheme, though yellow, yellow-green, white and lavender-blue flowers and bronze and yellow-green foliage abound.

Again, in the Lower Courtyard there is no colour scheme. However, here the effect is altogether different, with fewer, larger plants: we see each individual grouping as a separate episode rather than taking in the overall impression of a tapestry of varied colours and forms. The lack of a colour scheme might seem to make life easy; however, it can be harder to make every association pleasing than when a restricted colour range is used and every bloom automatically harmonizes with every other.

Throughout the garden at Sissinghurst, harmonies predominate and contrasts tend to be subtly pleasing rather than jarringly arresting. This may be because so many of the areas of the garden were used by Harold and Vita for repose, perhaps especially the White Garden where they dined in the fading light and the Cottage Garden where Harold sat by the door surveying Vita's sunset-coloured flowers. This approach might appeal to many gardeners, saving the most dramatic colour schemes for areas not meant for repose, perhaps parts of the garden seen *en passant* or acting as an appetizer for a more tranquil scheme.

Harmonies are generally created by combining colours that are close to each other in the spectrum, the main exception being that colours to either side of primary red, such as magenta and vermilion or crimson and scarlet, will clash with each other. This effect can limit what is planted on a brick-red wall, though those at Sissinghurst are a mellow, dull red that clashes with hardly any colour. The same phenomenon can also be used to create vibrant contrasts, for instance a cloud of tiny vermilion flowers set above a more solid display of larger, magenta blooms. The closest harmonies can seem dull and risk camouflaging the individual plants unless varied form and flower size are used.

For any colour scheme to 'read', at least a third, and preferably more than half, of its component plants should perform at the intended season. In Vita's day, the garden was organized so that each area had a short season when almost everything would flower. However, there was too little late summer or autumn display for most colour schemes to remain effective then. Pam and Sibylle recall that on their first visit on 17 July 1959, Vita told them, 'When I see the [*Alstroemeria*] *ligtu* hybrids, I know the season is over.' They took this as a challenge to make the garden as full of flower in the latter half of the year as it was earlier. This has suited the countless visitors to the garden, who, however unreasonably, expect every part of the garden to be full of colour whenever they come. Pam and Sibylle always tried to extend the season of each garden room, adding longer-flowering plants and coloured foliage and – extra work but worth the effort – annuals and tender perennials.

LEFT The Purple Border in the Top Courtyard in high summer at the peak of its display. The colours range from magenta and mauve to lavender blue, tones that look rich in dull weather and in the light of the setting sun but can look sullen for much of the day if it is sunny. A mixture of pale and dark hues and varied flower shapes help to enliven the display, as do the scarlet hips of *Rosa* 'Geranium', though these have yet to reveal their contrasting colour.

OVERLEAF A view into the Purple Border showing fragrant lupin 'Blue Jacket' and sweet rocket with the bold foliage of cardoons behind.

LEFT In spite of its name, the flowers of *Rosa* 'Geranium' are soft cherry red rather than the vibrant scarlet of a pelargonium. They are still distinct enough to contrast with the Purple Border's other colours.

RIGHT Vinous-purple *Allium sphaerocephalon*, magenta liatris and lythrum occupy the red end of the Purple Border's colour spectrum, while *Salvia* × *superba* is near the centre of its range. *Clematis* 'Perle d'Azur' and sweet pea 'Noel Sutton' are at the blue end; silvery *Eryngium* × *tripartitum* will turn steely blue as the inflorescences age. The spikes of salvia, lythrum and liatris contrast with the globes of the onion and the more diffuse habit of the eryngium.

ABOVE Though vines and other wall plants add variety and handsome foliage to the wall backing the Purple Border, it is the many clematis such as 'Perle d'Azur' here that fill the vital role of continuing the border's colour theme upwards.

RIGHT Using flowers of different sizes can create a more interesting tapestry: here, the tiny, dusky flowers of Viticella clematis 'Léonidas' mingle with the much larger, brighter ones of 'Madame Julia Correvon'.

In the Cottage Garden, by using tulips interplanted among late-leafing herbaceous plants, and wallflowers in spaces where summer bedding will follow, it is possible to have a blaze of spring colour in an area planted primarily for summer and autumn display, using the same hot colours. However, the delights of this part of the garden in spring do not depend on flowers alone. The low patchwork of foliage is never more attractive than in mid- to late spring with its variety of textures and shades of green. In the foreground are felted mulleins, chartreuse spears of crocosmia, bronzed fennel and spurge and fern-like poppies. Beyond lie the grassy glaucous leaves of asphodel and boldly pleated *Veratrum nigrum*.

LEFT An early display of wallflowers, tulips and other spring flowers. Sufficient quantities establish an interplay of colours from group to group, with tulip 'Georgette', maroon-purple 'Black Parrot' tulips and *Euphorbia polychroma* 'Major'. Behind are wallflower 'Vulcan', *Trollius* × *cultorum* 'Superbus' and Siberian wallflowers; by the cottage is the border wallflower 'Fire King'.

BELOW At the awkward moment when flowers are temporarily scarce, between the bountiful times of spring and summer, Intermediate Bearded irises such as 'Curlew' are useful to 'bridge the gap'. Here in the Cottage Garden they are accompanied by Siberian wallflowers (the latest sort for spring bedding) and hybrid columbines.

BELOW *Kniphofia* 'Royal Standard', a reliable poker flower surviving from Vita's time, not only contributes to what she described as 'the range of colours you might find in a sunset' but also brings height to the beds in mid- to late summer.

RIGHT The Cottage Garden shows how to use foliage to the full, providing a tapestry of pleasing shapes in gently varied shades of green that is never more attractive than in mid-spring. Plants should be chosen for their shape and texture as well as for their colour. Here woolly verbascums, full of the promise of a spectacular starburst, contrast with delicate columbines and have the added value that they will grow to a prodigious size.

The tower seen from the Cottage Garden with mulleins, coreopsis and dahlias.
The mulleins, whose vertical accents echo those of the tower and the Irish yews,
are Sissinghurst's own hybrid seed strain, raised from seed in the nursery and
planted in the Cottage Garden in autumn. Derived mainly from *Verbascum
olympicum* or *V. bombyciferum*, they are selected to have exceptional whiteness,
vigour and a generously branched inflorescence, ensuring a long-lasting display.

Canna indica 'Purpurea' is represented in gardens by several different clones with flowers in orange or red and with foliage more or less flushed purple. Its darkest-leaved variants do not share the magical translucency of this subtly shaded, thin-leaved clone from whose ramrod flower stems unfurl warm orange blooms, creating an ensemble of tropical luxuriance and exoticism.

LEFT Sunny colours abound as spring passes into summer, allowing an interplay of flower shapes in shades of yellow. Plates of *Achillea* 'Coronation Gold' and domed heads of *Euphorbia pilosa* 'Major' in yellow-green contrast with spires of tree lupin (*Lupinus arboreus*) and silvery verbascum stems.

BELOW The montbretia (*Crocosmia × crocosmiiflora*) cultivars play an invaluable role from midsummer to late autumn, with flowers ranging from butter yellow through orange to scarlet borne above elegantly arching grassy foliage. *C. × c.* 'Lady Hamilton' is one of several that are stalwarts in the Cottage Garden.

LEFT Apricot-orange flowers of *Lilium henryi*, an elegant, persistent and long-flowering species, are joined here by sulphur-yellow blooms of *Verbascum* Harkness hybrids and goldenrod in front of *Canna indica* 'Purpurea'.

ABOVE *Dahlia* 'David Howard' is one of the finest dark-leaved cultivars, with blooms of a soft, light orange whose inner shadows seem to glow with a deeper, richer tone. Other dahlias here include 'Autumn Lustre' in rich but gentle orange and pale lemon-yellow 'Glorie van Heemstede'.

The Cottage Garden contains red flowers of every shade between primary red and orange, including, in this Rousseauesque planting, the tawny sunflower 'Velvet Queen' and the bricky tints of *Salvia confertiflora*. Here in late autumn, yellow and yellow-green provide contrast, with *Euphorbia sikkimensis* in the foreground and *Sinacalia tangutica* (syn. *Senecio tanguticus*) and zebra grass behind, while beyond lie the vermilion blooms of *Canna indica* 'Purpurea' and the two-tone flowers of *Dahlia* 'Brandaris'.

A view along one of the
White Garden's cross-
axes to the statue of the
little virgin. The arbour's
Rosa mulliganii is in full
bloom, its fragrance
heavy on the air. Here is
some of the garden's
most symphonic
planting: foliage and
flowers harmonize with
each of their neighbours
in a succession of
satisfying associations.
The concerted effect
depends as much on the
subtle interplay of foliage
in shades of green as it
does on flowers. Here are
the greys of thistles,
artemisia and ajania,
glaucous lyme grass and
melianthus and the
puckered glossy leaves of
crambe in the deepest
green. Biennial
onopordum, already
adding height, and Miss
Willmott's ghost are
repeated around the
garden as a leitmotif.

In this oblique view from the Bishops' Gate towards the way through the yew hedge into the Orchard (top right), the path from the statue of the virgin to the seat lies hidden behind *Hosta* 'Royal Standard', *Paeonia lactiflora* 'Cheddar Gold', *Artemisia absinthium* 'Lambrook Silver', *Gillenia trifoliata* and Siberian iris 'White Swirl'. Throughout the planting, there is a balance between flower shapes and sizes and foliage colours and textures. Beyond the path are *Rosa pimpinellifolia* 'Double White', spires of lupin 'Noble Maiden', onopordums, single rose 'White Wings' and clouds of *Crambe cordifolia*.

LEFT, ABOVE *Rosa* Iceberg was planted here only months after Vita's death. Pruned less severely than is usual for a Floribunda, its bushes achieve an imposing size and flower almost continually, though they need protecting against blackspot.

LEFT, BELOW *Tanacetum parthenium* 'Rowallane' is the most floriferous but most miffy of feverfews. It must be cut back hard in August if it is to produce both cuttings for next year's plants and an autumn show.

RIGHT The relatively hardy arum lily *Zantedeschia aethiopica* 'Crowborough' requires little attention from year to year and produces blooms of superlative quality.

BELOW, LEFT *Cosmos bipinnatus* 'White Sensation', with its boss of lively yellow anthers, in front of *Rosa* Iceberg. The cosmos is grown from a late sowing under glass to replace white honesty and flowers until the frosts.

BELOW, RIGHT *Lilium regale* with seedheads of sea kale and *Lychnis coronaria* 'Alba'. The golden anthers and rosy tints on the lily buds and petal backs add warmth. The bold, clean lines of the lily flowers demonstrate the importance to design of floral form.

RIGHT The pale greyish-lilac of *Campanula* 'Burghaltii' stands out against gold-anthered *Rosa mulliganii* and complements the cool tints of silver-green-leaved *Artemisia pontica* and silvery blue-green *Eryngium maritimum*.

LEFT A cloud of creamy blooms of *Macleaya cordata* contrasts in floral form with the bold, starry flowers of *Clematis* 'John Huxtable', its pure white sepals surrounding cream anthers.

RIGHT, ABOVE The goat's rue *Galega* × *hartlandii* 'Alba' has spires of tiny pea flowers, each emerging greenish-cream and ageing to almost pure white.

RIGHT, BELOW *Thalictrum aquilegiifolium* 'White Cloud' has no petals but white filaments carrying yellow anthers, giving a creamy effect. This variety was chosen by Sissinghurst's gardeners for its exceptionally thick, white and long filaments, making it far more showy.

BELOW The bluish-green filigree foliage of *Tanacetum ptarmiciflorum* contrasts gently with the pale lemon-centred flowers of *Argyranthemum* 'Qinta White'. The marguerite needs short stakes worked through its base to support its sappy stems and heavy flowers.

RIGHT An oblique glimpse across the White Garden to the little virgin in the bluish light of dusk, with the feverfew and marguerite (below) seen at the bottom right. Other silvers include *Lychnis coronaria* 'Alba' and weeping silver pear (*Pyrus salicifolia* 'Pendula').

As the days grow shorter and the frosts approach, tints of red and fawn add interest: the tiny hips of *Rosa mulliganii* on the arbour are echoed below by scarlet-flushed leaves of *Rosa pimpinellifolia* 'Double White'. Glaucous *Melianthus major* has perhaps the most handsome late-season foliage. Beyond it, *Leucanthemella serotina* (syn. *Chrysanthemum uliginosum*) is invaluable for its late flowers, while beyond the arbour *Cosmos bipinnatus* 'White Sensation' flowers bravely until the frosts.

LEFT The seedheads of grasses, like *Pennisetum villosum* here, can remain attractive through autumn and well into winter. *Chrysanthemum* 'Anastasia' behind and shrubby *Caryopteris* × *clandonensis* in front also provide valuable late display.

RIGHT Seedheads of *Allium cristophii* add long-lasting interest beneath *Anemone* × *hybrida* 'Honorine Jobert', a useful and beautiful Japanese anemone for midsummer to late autumn bloom.

Meadow and Woodland Ground Cover

Spring Woodlanders

Late Spring Flowers

Meadow Grasses

Meadow Bulbs

In the Nuttery, at the foot of a young god gazing stonily from his plinth, a millefleurs carpet, recalling Botticelli's *Primavera*, or Burne-Jones, is woven from a thousand wildflowers and woodlanders, some native, some not.

Though the culture of flowery meadows and of woodland ground cover may seem quite different, they share common features. Both cover substantial areas with low-maintenance planting. Both rely on plants being of comparable vigour to their neighbours and ecologically suited to their site and its management. Their decorative success depends on creating a tapestry of interwoven plants.

In Sissinghurst's Nuttery, the carpet of polyanthus that astonished visitors in the 1950s and 1960s but proved impossible to grow was replaced in 1975 by a tapestry of woodlanders, flowers, ferns and grasses, longer lasting, more subtle and in many ways more delightful than the previous bright bedding. Even throughout summer and autumn, the intermingling pattern of foliage, fruits and fewer flowers remains charming and richly varied. This is ground-cover planting at its best, easy to maintain, diverse and suited in character and in scale to its setting,

In the Orchard (essentially a meadow with added fruit trees), naturalized bulbs, wildflowers and shimmering grasses flourish; their success depends on precisely judged and timed maintenance. Many of us plant spring bulbs beneath grass and know that mowing must wait until the bulb foliage dies back. Adding autumn-flowering bulbs further limits the mowing season. If wildflowers too are to bloom and compete successfully with the grass, the sward cannot be cut until they have shed their seed; the fertility of the ground must be low, reduced usually by many years of removing all grass clippings. All these requirements are taken into account at Sissinghurst to achieve a regime that is relatively labour-saving and creates a charmingly informal effect, a contrast to more brightly coloured and highly cultivated areas of the garden.

Vita began planting bulbs in the Orchard's turf soon after she and Harold moved to Sissinghurst. Her snowdrops, *Crocus tommasinianus*, snakeshead fritillaries, colchicums and narcissi survive. The daffodils are now almost too abundant, the beauty of the individuals in peril of being lost through the sheer density and number of their flowers. Fortunately there are enough cream and white varieties to leaven the many yellows and to avoid a too even carpet of colour. But to some, the Orchard's greatest glory is not the braying trumpets of daffodils but the haze of misty blue cast by *Veronica filiformis*, studded with golden stars of celandines and dandelions.

The mowing regime suits all the flowering plants in the turf, allowing bulb foliage to die back and wildflowers such as oxeye daisies to seed. The grass is cut as late as possible in autumn or early winter, just as the daffodils start to nose through the ground, so that their clumps of blooms will stand clear above tidy sward for maximum effect. Thereafter only the paths are mown until late July, when a rear-discharge rotary mower cuts the whole Orchard to about 5cm/2in, picking up all the long grass.

The mowing regime allows the intricate tapestry of grass flowers to be enjoyed to the full, with waving heads in shades of fawn, soft sage green, russet and dusky purple, a subtle and delightful display. A further cut is needed on 19 August, about two days before the first flowers of *Colchicum byzantinum* appear. Many different colchicums have been added over the years, chosen to give a succession of bloom into the autumn. They are occasionally divided as the leaves die back, preventing the bulbs producing a series of tight and evenly sized blobs of blossom. There are also some naturalized autumn-flowering *Crocus speciosus*, another element in a scheme that ensures beauty and interest from late winter until the following fall.

Wood anemones, oxlips and *Viola riviniana* 'Purpurea' appear with emerging shoots of *Polygonatum odoratum* 'Variegatum'. In the Nuttery's scheme of 'greenery-yallery', blue and white, plants are mixed and mingled as though placed by nature. There is no struggling with problem plants: there are plenty of suitable subjects that survive happily without becoming too invasive or dwindling away, so there is no need for cosseting, frequent division or reduction of groups. An annual mulch of crushed bark helps suppress weeds and tops up the humus content of the soil.

BELOW The bold foliage of *Rheum palmatum* 'Atrosanguineum', with Mrs Robb's bonnet (*Euphorbia amygdaloides* var. *robbiae*), *Epimedium × youngianum* 'Niveum' and white Spanish bluebells. The euphorbia soon dies where it is put and moves on elsewhere but its handsome rosettes of deep green leaves topped with showy chartreuse inflorescences are welcome wherever they choose to appear.

RIGHT White wood anemones and *Epimedium × youngianum* 'Niveum', nestling at the foot of a filbert, add lightness and grace to the carpet of foliage and flowers.

The Nuttery's planting is most successful where two or three plants are combined that grow at similar rates, co-exist contentedly and complement each other beautifully. Mixtures such as *Onoclea sensibilis* with *Smyrnium perfoliatum,* ABOVE, or with white bluebells, RIGHT, or Bowles' golden grass (*Milium effusum* 'Aureum') with wood anemones and white bluebells, OVERLEAF, are not happy accidents but carefully contrived and skilfully managed feats of the gardener's art.

Woodlanders that are slow to spread, such as orchids and, here, *Trillium grandiflorum*, are divided periodically to make impressive drifts of a size seen in few other gardens in the British Isles. The temptation to be greedy with such treasures, making a drift so large and dense that it disturbs the scale and balance of the rest of the planting, must be avoided and they are planted in a loosely scattered manner that imitates nature. The elegant lines and bold shape of the trillium flowers make a striking statement among less dramatic neighbours, including *Omphalodes cappadocica*, Welsh poppies (*Meconopsis cambrica*) and polyanthus.

LEFT After the spring bulbs have finished, grass flowers add texture, movement and subtle colour to the sward beneath the Orchard's fruit trees.

ABOVE Close-mown paths encourage visitors to the outermost corner of the Orchard, where the gazebo, Nigel Nicolson's memorial to his father, looks across rolling countryside towards Canterbury.

BELOW After being mown in July and August, the grass forms a fresh green short sward, a perfect foil for *Colchicum agrippinum*.

RIGHT *Elaeagnus* 'Quicksilver', blue *Symphytum caucasicum*, and *Narcissus poeticus* in bloom in the Orchard.

Roses Old and New

Roses Old and New

Summer Companions

Training Roses

Climbers and Ramblers

In the Long Border, *Allium cristophii* jostles with blooms of Bourbon rose 'Prince Charles'.

O f all Sissinghurst's flowers, it was the roses that most captured Vita's imagination, their colours sumptuous or delicate, their textures of velvet or satin, with evocative fragrance and glorious blooms borne in early summer. The science and art of pruning and training roses have developed to exemplary standards at Sissinghurst over the years. So too has the companion planting, chosen both to compliment the roses and to extend the season of display.

Vita's roses are central to Sissinghurst's style of planting and typical of its soft abundance, subtlety and romance. However, as Vita admitted, 'they have one major fault . . . their flowering period is limited to one glorious month of midsummer. Personally I think they are more than worth it.' With a few exceptions, the roses here are of three types. First and foremost are the old roses, Gallicas, Damasks, Centifolias, Albas, Hybrid Perpetuals and Bourbons, in plush crimson-purples, satin pinks and extravagant stripes. It is these colours along with the amethyst tints of alliums that dominate the Rose Garden to this day. To these were added Hybrid Musks, valued for their fragrance and recurrent bloom, and a small but select handful of Hybrid Tea and Floribunda roses, chosen for exquisite form and colouring. Though a similar effect could be achieved using more modern varieties such as the English roses raised by David Austin, the varieties at Sissinghurst remain those grown by Vita, an unchanging element of the garden.

At Sissinghurst, staking, pruning and retraining are completed by early winter so that other work on the beds can be started without the hindrance of wayward rose stems. The gardeners have never found resultant frost damage to young shoots to be a problem. All dead and weak old wood plus spindly young growths are pruned away and remaining stems are shortened.

Many roses are trained to hazel 'benders', long straight boughs that are grown for the purpose. Originally these were used to train the roses almost flat on the ground, but the technique was adapted by the gardeners to produce dome-shaped, well-clad bushes of varied heights, anchoring the lowest rose stems to the benders and building up the dome with the stems of the rose itself. Other roses, quite short cultivars such as *Rosa gallica* 'Versicolor' as well as more vigorous varieties, are trained to three or four vertical sweet chestnut poles. The bush roses and a few of the short shrub varieties (for example 'Leda', 'Nuits de Young' and *R. gallica* var. *officinalis*) need no support. Once pruning, staking and tying have been completed, the gardeners work systematically through the beds, digging areas to be replanted and mulching with fine crushed bark as they go.

Irises were important companions for the roses from the start. Many of Harold and Vita's irises remain, especially the Tall Bearded cultivars, their blooming coinciding with that of the roses and their spiky foliage providing contrasting form. Lilies continued the garden's display for a few precious weeks of high summer. Other survivors from Harold and Vita's time include Japanese anemones, pinks and *Alchemilla mollis*, whose chartreuse provided a piquant contrast for pink and dusky purple roses.

For late summer, the gardeners have added achilleas, agapanthus, asters, cranesbills, catmints and campanulas, many of them starting into bloom with the roses but continuing in flower long after. Half-hardy perennials such as salvias and a few annuals such as *Nicotiana* 'Lime Green' are valued for their long and showy flowering season. On the walls, clematis extend the display upwards and into the autumn while, beneath the roses, colchicum blooms push through low carpeting plants such as bugles to give yet more late colour.

Vita wrote of 'the need . . . to welcome the less familiar purples and lilacs, and the striped, flaked, mottled variations' among the old roses. Perhaps especially she loved the most richly and deeply coloured among them, such as the sumptuous and velvety Moss 'Nuits de Young', seen here LEFT foreground, with bright carmine Hybrid Musk 'Vanity' and striped Rosa Mundi in the background. The unusual Hybrid Perpetual 'Baron Girod de l'Ain', RIGHT ABOVE, is another example, as is, RIGHT BELOW, the Gallica 'Sissinghurst Castle' a variety of unknown origin found when Harold and Vita came to Sissinghurst and grown in beds in the Orchard.

LEFT Much the brightest of the varieties in the Rose Garden, the Hybrid Musk 'Vanity' is valuable, like others of its class, for its recurrent bloom. Its companions here are amethyst *Allium cernuum* 'Hidcote' and an ivory selection of *Sparaxis fragrans* subsp. *grandiflora*.

RIGHT 'Felicia', like 'Vanity', is another Hybrid Musk raised by the Revd Joseph Pemberton in the years shortly before Harold and Vita came to Sissinghurst. Its delicate flesh pink, informal blooms are sweetly scented.

BELOW The lilac flowerheads of *Allium cristophii*, a species grown here by Harold and Vita, interact effectively with the lowest branches of the roses and are followed by globes of parchment-coloured starry seedpods.

RIGHT The Texensis clematis 'Etoile Rose' provides a contrast of floral form with the Rambler rose 'Albertine' and continues to furnish the Rose Garden wall with bloom long after the rose has finished.

RIGHT In a magical plant association devised by the gardeners, spires of *Digitalis purpurea* f. *albiflora* and *D.p.* 'Sutton's Apricot' shine against the blush flowers and deep bronze leaves of *Sambucus nigra* 'Guincho Purple' and palest lemon-cream Hybrid Musk rose 'Pax'. About a third of the elder stems are cut out each year, keeping a balance between good foliage and abundant flower. The foxgloves are removed the moment the peak of their display is over, to be replaced with gentian blue *Salvia cacaliifolia* and silver *Helichrysum petiolare*.

OVERLEAF The white standards of lupin 'Blue Jacket' provide sparkle against its richly sombre violet-blue keels; the blooms of the single apricot Hybrid Tea rose 'Mrs Oakley Fisher' unfurl from elegant buds, providing a perfect contrast.

ABOVE Several bushes of the same variety have been trained to hazel benders to produce a dome of moderate height. Varieties with nodding blooms such as 'Madame Lauriol de Barny' are trained higher so that their blooms can be seen from beneath.

RIGHT More lax Climbing roses, Ramblers and some Bourbons produce abundant flowering laterals if trained spirally around vertical supports, occasionally taking one or two stems over the top to clothe it adequately.

Climbing roses and
Ramblers are used in
almost all of Sissinghurst's
garden rooms to clothe
the walls. Ramblers,
being more lax, slender
and flexible, can be used
in a more informal way
than their stiffer cousins
the Climbing roses, as in
the Orchard, LEFT, where
the richly perfumed
Sempervirens Rambler
'Félicité Perpétue' drapes
itself elegantly through
an old pear tree. This
same laxness allows them
to be trained tightly to
structures such as the
White Garden's arbour,
RIGHT, where *Rosa
mulliganii* provides a
spectacular display
each July.

Garden Structure and Ornament

Framing with Yew

Box Edging

Dramatic Containers

Well-placed Seats

In the Herb Garden, the seat that marks the focal point of one of the cross-axes is seen behind old man, birthwort, foxgloves and the seedheads of Pasque flower. This seat, like all the wooden benches at Sissinghurst, was made of oak, so that it would age to an attractive silver. A design with a wavy top was chosen because a straight top might have drawn attention to the sloping hedge behind.

M uch of the success of Sissinghurst is due to the way that each garden room seems satisfyingly complete and rectilinear, with its own vistas and focal points. It seems as though Harold and Vita merely joined up the dots to recreate a pre-existing picture of garden perfection. This is an illusion, for although almost every surviving fragment of old Sissinghurst was worked into the design, before Harold and Vita came there were no vistas, only the tower and entrance arch as focal points, and most of the rooms had only three of their four sides. The remaining wall might have been placed anywhere, at Vita's or, more usually, Harold's whim. And at Sissinghurst, right angles are rare. That the finished result seems so unforced and so logical is no accident but a testament to the skill of their design.

Of the walls that were added to complete each of the rooms, only a few were brick. More were yew or, around the perimeter of the garden, hornbeam, a coarser-textured and more naturalistic choice to be seen in conjunction with the countryside beyond, both of them cheaper than bricks and mortar and often a more pleasing foil for flowers.

Each of the garden's rooms was given a focus using traditional elements of garden design such as a statue, seat or vase, often placed to serve two axes so that the barest minimum was needed. Thus the statue of Dionysus terminates the vista from the entrance arch through the tower, as well as that along the Moat Walk; the bacchante statue is seen both at the end of the vista across the Rose Garden's rondel and at the head of the Lime Walk; and the Cottage Garden's Irish yews also crown the vista along the Moat Walk.

The addition of these few well-chosen items as focal points, bringing with them the romance of the past, is made all the more telling by the simplicity of the framework that contains them. Jane Brown in *Sissinghurst: Portrait of a Garden* has identified the garden's restraint as a noteworthy feature: 'Along with the plethora of imitations of the English classical revival style come a whole host of familiar furnishings, which it is well to note that Sissinghurst does *not* have: it has no long grass walk flanked by double borders, no pergola, no pools or fountains, no trellis walks or arbours and no topiary twists or triangles. . . . There is no iris rill nor laburnum tunnel, no balustraded terrace or columned temple, and there are very definitely no Japanese touches or *trompe l'œil* effects. There are plenty of such things in other gardens.' All the hedges were flat-topped and, except for the buttresses in the Herb Garden, without any piers or finials.

Plants could have been used to punctuate minor axes within each garden room, perhaps an exclamation mark of phormium or yucca, or a fountain of pampas grass. This was not Vita's style: her planting was always soft and billowing, never crudely emphatic. The Cottage Garden's yews are perhaps the only plants used as focal points. It may be through Vita's influence that the garden is so restrained; she sometimes dismissed Harold's more imaginative suggestions in favour of something simpler. Only in the box parterre of the White Garden, the yew buttresses of the Herb Garden and perhaps the design of Sissinghurst Crescent is there any adornment, anything other than the most basic and elemental treatment possible. There are more ornamental gewgaws and hard landscaping in the average television makeover of a small garden than there are in the whole of Sissinghurst. It is a tribute to Harold's skill that so many who visit Sissinghurst today find it so logical that it is hard to believe its enclosures and axes were not always there. There are few aspects of the design that fail to satisfy completely.

LEFT Yew is the supreme hedging plant for shaping into crisp and imposing architecture, the very structure of the garden, as here in the walls of the Yew Walk. Shafts of light across openings in the hedges and, acting as a focal point, a splendid stone vase encourage the visitor to explore.

RIGHT Sissinghurst's success depends largely on contrast between the strict architecture of Harold's paths and walls and the exuberant informality of Vita's planting. On the vista through the tower arch, across an opening in the Yew Walk and into the Orchard, structure is also defined by the walk's yew hedges and those of hornbeam on the far side of the Orchard. The ancient trees around the garden's perimeter add informality, while the whole ensemble is simply furnished by pots of hedychium and plecostachys, an elegant chandelier and the distant statue of Dionysus.

LEFT This view across the Rose Garden to the head of the Lime Walk uses exactly the same elements as the previous one from the tower arch, though the architecture of the yew rondel is even more imposing.

BELOW Four Irish yews, straddling the crossing of the Cottage Garden's axial paths, act as a combined focal point, for the view along the Moat Walk as well as here within the Cottage Garden itself. Their vertical shape is echoed by the stems of mulleins.

The half of the White Garden north of the arbour consists of a parterre of four matching quarters, each of them containing four L-shaped box-edged beds surrounding a box cube. The strong pattern of the beds and the crisply regular shape of hedges and cubes, softened only slightly by regrowth of the box, make a pleasing contrast to the effusive growth of some of the plants within the beds. **Iceberg** roses, *Cosmos bipinnatus* 'White Sensation', silver *Helichrysum petiolare* and *Artemisia arborescens* all billow over the top of the edging. The central brick path lacks box edging, allowing plants in the beds to tumble over the path, further softening the effect, and the relative flatness of the scheme is relieved by the two Perpendicular arches, echoing the same shapes within the arbour. The box chosen here is not yellowish-green-leaved edging box, *Buxus sempervirens* 'Suffruticosa', but several bluish-green clones of common box. These give a slight but pleasing variation in colour and texture within the hedges. Clipping is not possible at the preferred season (late summer or early autumn) when the garden is open to the public, so is done in mid-autumn.

Against a sunny wall in the Top Courtyard, a stone sink adds interest as a home for a superlative auricula.

The same sink planted for summer display with *Osteospermum* 'White Pim'.

LEFT Pots of choice and
tender plants are brought
out from the glasshouses
when in flower and used
on the tower steps or by
the Bishops' Gate. Perhaps
the most remarkable of
these is the Chilean
relative of the pineapple,
Puya alpestris. Its strange
peacock green flowers
dripping with nectar are
borne only once every
two or three years.

RIGHT Handsome
Hedychium gardnerianum, a
relative of ginger, is not
quite hardy enough to
survive the winter in the
Cottage Garden but
performs well in pots on
the tower steps, furnished
beneath with variegated
Felicia amelloides.

Tall Ali Baba pots at either end of the Lime Walk and at intervals along it have been planted over the years with various subjects, most of them trailing plants such as clematis, *Lathyrus nervosus* or *Helichrysum petiolare*. Here in spring *Euphorbia characias* subsp. *wulfenii* makes a dramatic vertical accent, matching in colour the shorter *E. pilosa* 'Major' in the beds beneath.

Along the Lime Walk, the brilliant spring display of bulbs is followed by a simple rhythmic pattern of pots of *Impatiens walleriana* Blitz Series. The growth and covering of flowers on busy Lizzies such as these are absolutely even on both sunny and shady sides. Modern dwarf varieties would be too small to be effective here.

ABOVE The old laundry copper, a relic of Sissinghurst's days as a workhouse, has a blue-green colour that combines superbly with the soft orange flowers of *Mimulus aurantiacus*, a combination first used by Harold and Vita.

RIGHT The White Garden is glorious in early summer when *Rosa mulliganii* casts a canopy of fragrant bloom over the gothic arbour. The pot beneath holds greenish-cream-flowered *Clematis forsteri*. In the distance, pink martagon lilies bloom in Delos.

BELOW Created from fragments of the old house and christened Edward the Confessor's chair by Harold and Vita, the camomile seat is seen here in spring with spurge laurel and parsley pots.

RIGHT The chair in summer, well upholstered with non-flowering 'Treneague' camomile, behind white borage, biennial clary, lavender and 'Tricolor' sage.

OVERLEAF The Herb Garden in spring. The brick and stone paths were designed by Nigel Nicolson, to replace paths of concrete and grass. Harold and Vita brought the marble bowl supported by three lions from Cospoli in Turkey in 1914.

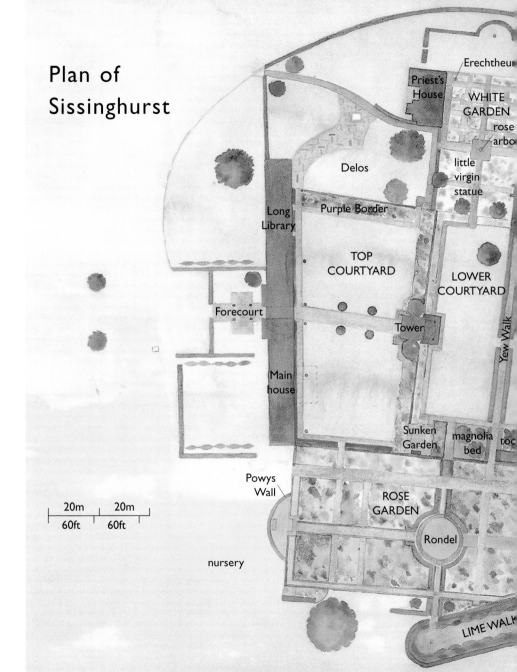

Plan of Sissinghurst

Erechtheu

Priest's House

WHITE GARDEN

rose arbo

Delos

little virgin statue

Long Library

Purple Border

TOP COURTYARD

LOWER COURTYARD

Forecourt

Tower

Yew Walk

Main house

Sunken Garden

magnolia bed

toc

Powys Wall

ROSE GARDEN

20m   20m
60ft   60ft

Rondel

nursery

LIME WALK

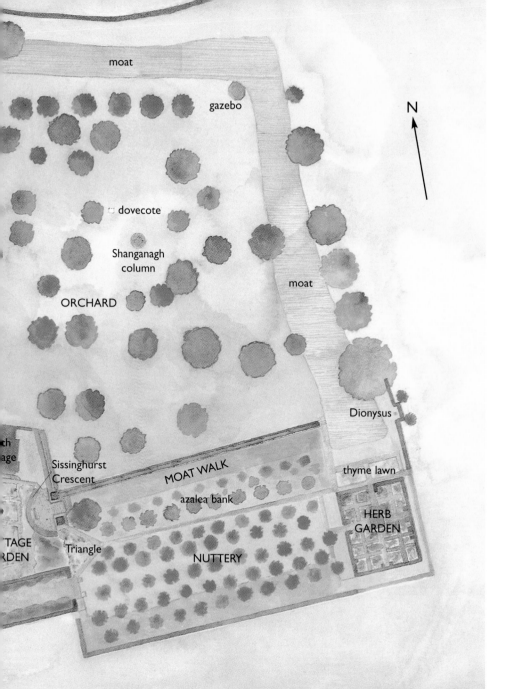

moat

gazebo

N

dovecote

Shanganagh
column

ORCHARD

moat

Dionysus

Sissinghurst
Crescent

MOAT WALK

thyme lawn

azalea bank

HERB
GARDEN

TAGE
RDEN

Triangle

NUTTERY

Index

Publishers' Acknowledgments

Design by Caroline Hillier

Editor Anne Askwith

Production Kim Oliver

Index by Margot Levy

Watercolour plan by Nicky Cooney